FOCUS ON THE FAMILY®

A Child Is a Precious Gift

Paintings by

KATHRYN ANDREWS FINCHER

HARVEST HOUSE PUBLISHERS

EUGENE, OREGON

A Child Is a Precious Gift

(Formerly Heaven Sent)

Copyright © 1999 Focus on the Family®
Published by Harvest House Publishers
Eugene, Oregon 97402

Focus on the Family® is a registered trademark of Focus on the Family, Colorado Springs, CO 80995.
For more information, please contact:

Focus on the Family
Colorado Springs, CO 80995
1-800-A-Family
www.family.org

Artwork designs are reproduced under license from © Arts Uniq'®, Inc., Cookeville, TN and may not be reproduced
without permission. For information regarding art prints featured in this book, please contact:

Arts Uniq'
P.O. Box 3085
Cookeville TN 38502
800-223-5020

Library of Congress Cataloging-in-Publication Data
A child is a precious gift / Focus on the Family; paintings by Kathryn Andrews Fincher.
   p. cm.
   ISBN 0-7369-0864-1
   1. Children—Quotations, maxims, etc. 2. Child rearing—Quotations, maxims, etc.
   I. Fincher, Kathryn Andrews. II. Focus on the Family (Organization)

PN6084.C5.C48 2002
305.23—dc21   2002022709

Design and Production by Koechel Peterson and Associates, Inc., Minneapolis, Minnesota

"Amazing Grace" is from *The Strong-Willed Child* by Dr. James Dobson, © 1978 by Tyndale House Publishers, Inc.
Used by permission. All rights reserved.

"Big Sister" is from *Parenting Isn't for Cowards* by James T. Dobson, © 1987, Word Publishing, Nashville, Tennessee. All rights reserved.

"Hail to the Chief" is from *Children at Risk* by James T. Dobson and Gary L. Bauer, © 1990, Word Publishing, Nashville,
Tennessee. All rights reserved.

Focus on the Family® and Harvest House Publishers have made every effort to trace the ownership of all anecdotes, poems,
and quotes. In the event of a question arising from the use of any anecdote, poem, or quote, we regret any error made
and will be pleased to make the necessary correction in future editions of this book.

Scripture quotations are from the Holy Bible, New International Version®, Copyright © 1973, 1978, 1984 by the International
Bible Society. Used by permission of Zondervan Publishing House.

Printed in Hong Kong.

02 03 04 05 06 07 08 09 10 11 /NG/ 10 9 8 7 6 5 4 3 2

CHILDREN ARE LIVING JEWELS
dropped unsustained from heaven.
—Robert Pollok

heaven   *living*

jewels

Gifts from Above

If the best kind of gifts are blessings to both giver and receiver, then children certainly must be the best gift of all. Like the angels of heaven, little ones live with the purpose to make life gentler and cheerier to those around them. From the very start, children have a natural tendency to be helpers, always ready to attempt to lift the heaviest bag of groceries or determined to patch up a disagreement between friends. Through their selfless and loving actions, children certainly mirror the heart of their Creator, seeking to make life's responsibilities a little less heavy and life's friendships a little more sweet. Blessing others through their eagerness to lend a helping hand, children are the best kind of gift from above.

children are the best kind of gift from above

EACH CHILD IS CREATED IN THE SPECIAL IMAGE AND LIKENESS OF GOD
for greater things— to love and be loved.

—Mother Teresa

5

Mommy's Helper

As we were driving home one afternoon, my daughter Eleanor started talking to her little brother seated beside her in his car seat. She sang little songs for him. She went through "Rudolph, the Red-Nosed Reindeer," "Jingle Bells," and "Jesus Loves Me." Then she started singing, "It's raining, it's snowing, the old man is snoring." She paused. "Austin," she asked her little brother very seriously, "do you know why the old man couldn't get up in the morning? It's because he bumped his head. Do you bump your head sometimes, Austin?" She had him so happy in his car seat.

When we got home, I thanked her for all the help she'd been to me. She got this wide-eyed look like, "Did I really help, Mom?" followed by a big smile on her face.

"You're welcome," was all she said.

—Mendy Griffith

OF ALL CREATED THINGS,
the loveliest and most divine are children.

—William Canton

A Heartfelt Gift

My adventurous young daughter always loved animals. We lived in a townhouse complex at the time, and we had tadpoles all over the place. Tadpoles are a real joy to watch, but those tadpoles soon become adult frogs. One day I heard a knock on the door, and I peeked out and noticed it was my child trying to get back into the house.

"You know how to open the door," I said to her. "You don't need me to open it for you."

"Oh, yes, I do. My hands are full."

When I opened the door, she was standing there, greeting me with two frogs that she was ready to drop at my feet. I began to tell her that she could not bring those frogs into the house, but she interrupted me.

"But, Mommy, I've given them to everyone down the block."

Not sure what to expect, I asked her to explain.

"I've put two frogs in everyone's mailbox."

As the neighbors came home that day, I could hear them all outside talking. "Have the frogs started invading your house? This is so strange!"

My little girl was very proud of the gifts she had given the entire neighborhood that day.

—Anonymous

A Present of Love

My children have always been such a blessing. Recently, we've had rough times financially. I had bills to pay and no money to pay them with. My young kids went upstairs, collected the money from their piggy banks, and brought it down to me. With hugs and kisses they said, "Mom, you don't have to pay us back. This is our present of love. This is our gift to you."

Their gesture of love made me cry. We just held each other. They showed me how unselfish and giving their love really is.

—Anonymous

CHILDREN ARE A GIFT FROM GOD;
they are His reward.
—The Book of Psalms

Simple Pleasures

Children naturally know how to live a life of simplicity. They find delight in the traditional yet uncomplicated pleasures of youth. From mud puddles to mud pies, children appreciate the usefulness of the surrounding world. Though the price of a glass has risen from a penny to a quarter, a lemonade stand still provides a full day of entertainment and enterprise. Come Christmas, many little ones prefer the boxes and wrapping paper to the gift itself. A child can spend hours watching cloud formations float by in the afternoon breeze. Children instinctively know that a cat sidling up to them on the sidewalk needs to be petted for a full ten minutes. And both child and kitty will scamper off to their next adventure feeling much better for having taken the time.

A CHILD'S LIFE HAS NO DATES, IT IS FREE, SILENT, DATELESS.
A child's life ought to be a child's life, full of simplicity.
—Oswald Chambers

A Child's Delight

Suzanne and I were lying at the beach with our journals, and we got to watching this child. She was about three years old, and she had little pigtails sticking out like little handles on the side of her head. She would run down and chase the tide as it went out, and she'd run as fast as her little legs would carry her and race back up the beach, trying to see if she could get to the top of the tide before it hit her in the backside. She always lost, of course. The tide came faster than she could run. Every time it would hit her and knock her down and the water would splash around her, she would just laugh the most contagious laugh that would ripple through the air, all up and down the beach.

Pretty soon, everybody was watching this incredible child, and everybody at the beach laughed when that little girl got hit every time. All of us were involved with this child because she was us. She was doing what we all wanted to do. Suzanne and I watched until finally the sun was down. We folded our stuff and went in, and she was still running at the waves when we left.

That night, Suzanne handed me what she had written in her journal:

*everybody was watching
this incredible child*

I saw her there.
As breaking waves
Dashed around her little feet
She laughed again
And dashed at them
Her eyes so full
She could not take it in
(Not all at once, at least)
But breathe she did
Until her tiny lungs
Would burst with all the air
Then wild laughter broke into the wind.
For hours it seemed
The waves and she
Played their little game.
The sun had set without her knowing
And as I turned to leave
I threw at her a final glance
At the pigtails dancing in the sand.
Oh, to throw myself at sea
And drown in the immensity
My wish to thrust into the waves
A simple trust,
    A simple joy,
        A simple love of simple days.

—Gloria Gaither

EACH DAY OF OUR LIVES WE MAKE DEPOSITS
in the memory banks of our children.
—Charles R. Swindoll

Messengers of Happiness

If it's a blue sort of day, you can almost always depend on a child to turn it the color of sunshine. Some children seem to instinctively know when a hug or a smile is needed, while others can always be depended on to tell a funny joke, make giggle–inducing faces, or cause roars of laughter simply by going about their daily business. Messengers of happiness, children twist common phrases and make up non–sense rhymes that have a genius all their own. Listen to these words and watch these antics, for in them you'll see glimpses of the person they are becoming and catch shades of deepest understanding. A missed deadline or a disappointing meeting begin to fade as you watch the children play, defining exactly what it means to find joy in the moment. Children know the gifts of today are precious, and they invite you to find happiness in their presence.

*children know the gifts
of today are precious*

I REMEMBER SEEING A PICTURE OF AN OLD MAN ADDRESSING A SMALL BOY. "HOW OLD ARE YOU?" "WELL, IF YOU GO BY WHAT MAMA SAYS, I'M FIVE. *But if you go by the fun I've had, I'm almost a hundred.*"

—William Lyons Phelps

Fish Food

When my daughter Sharon was five years old, she asked permission to feed the few fish that we kept in a goldfish bowl. Soon after, I heard her from the next room yelling, "No! Get back! Don't eat!"

She kept repeating this over and over. "No! Get back! Don't eat!"

I hurried in and asked her what the problem was. She was standing over the fishbowl, trying to shoo the fish away from the food.

"I don't want the fish to eat," she explained. "They haven't even said grace yet."

—Pat Trout

grace

find joy in the moment

WHERE CHILDREN ARE,
there is the golden age.
—Novalis

Amazing Grace

Since the time of his babyhood, my little two-year-old son had seen his sister, mother, and father say grace before eating our meals. But because of his age, we had never asked our little toddler to lead the prayer. On one occasion when I was gone, my wife put the lunch on the table and spontaneously turned to our boy and said, "Would you like to pray for our food today?"

Her unexpected request apparently startled him. He glanced around nervously, then clasped his little hands together and said, "I love you, Daddy. Amen."

—Dr. James Dobson

A WORLD WITHOUT CHILDREN IS A WORLD
without newness, regeneration, color, and vigor.
—Dr. James Dobson

Little Girls

Little girls have the ability to remember lots of things—the names, personality types, and voice inflections of dozens of stuffed animals and dolls, book plots and film scripts to act out on the stage of the front porch, each friend's favorite type of cookie to eat and game to play. Little girls turn swing sets into airplanes, small garden plots into vast expanses of field and farm, houses into giant ocean liners when it's raining outside. Taking friends and parents by the hand, little girls invite them to join them in the land of make-believe, insisting that it's a mere baby step from reality to fantasy. Delighting in the details and placing no limits on the possibilities, each day is a wide-open slate for the creative games of little girls.

creative

no limits on the possibilities

A GIRL IS INNOCENCE PLAYING IN THE MUD, BEAUTY STANDING ON ITS HEAD, *and Motherhood dragging a doll by the foot.*
—Allan Beck

Big Sister

A few months ago I was making several phone calls in the family room where my three-year-old daughter, Adrianne, and my five-month-old son, Nathan, were playing quietly. Nathan loves Adrianne, who has been learning how to mother him gently since the time of his birth.

I suddenly realized that the children were no longer in view. Panic-stricken, I quickly hung up the phone and went looking for the pieces. Down the hall and around the corner I found the children playing cheerfully in Adrianne's bedroom.

Relieved and upset, I shouted, "Adrianne, you know you are not allowed to carry Nathan! He is too little, and you could hurt him if he fell!"

Startled, she answered, "I didn't, Mommy."

Knowing he couldn't crawl, I suspiciously demanded, "Well, then, how did he get all the way into your room?"

Confident of my approval for her obedience, she said with a smile, "I rolled him!"

He is still alive, and they are still best friends.

—As told by Dr. James Dobson

MY DEAR LITTLE DAUGHTER, YOU ARE NOT REALLY SO LITTLE AS ALL THAT...BUT LIKE ALL REAL MOTHERS SINCE THE WORLD BEGAN, I STILL *think of you as little; and the sweetest thing God ever made.*

—Caitlin Thomas

Little Boys

There's something delightfully impish about little boys. Ask one what he did that day and he'll launch into an elaborate description of the dragons he slayed, the wild horses he tamed, the faraway lands he discovered. He'll tell you these tales with a twinkle in his eye, knowing that you don't entirely believe his exaggerations but wanting to impress all the same. And you listen, adding all the right exclamations— really? truly? amazing!—as your eyes grow big with curiosity. For in a sense, he did wrestle mythical beasts and venture into uncharted territory that day in the playground of his imagination. And he's returned to share the glory and wonder with those who anxiously awaited his safe journey home.

in the playground of his imagination

NO ONE IS GOING TO CATCH ME, LADY, AND MAKE ME A MAN.
I want always to be a little boy and to have fun.

—James M. Barrie
Peter Pan

23

Help Da Boy

I was home alone with my two-year-old son, and I suddenly realized it had been about two minutes since I had heard from Ryan. In our house, silence is not golden. When you haven't heard from Ryan, you go find out what he's into or what he's about to fall off of because he's a hazard to himself and to the whole family. His first question is, "How does it work?" and his second question is, "How can I destroy it?" I thought he was in his bedroom where I had seen him two or three minutes before. I went in there to see what he was doing, but Ryan was not there.

I saw that he had been there, so I followed the debris around into the living room, where I expected him to be, but he wasn't there either. I went in our bedroom, and he was not there. I went all over the house. In about two minutes' time that little two-year-old had managed to disappear. I was starting to panic because I could see him running down the middle of the freeway somewhere.

imagination

Finally, I went into the kitchen and looked through the kitchen window, out into the backyard where we have kind of a circular driveway. I saw that somehow Ryan had managed to go out the back door, down the steps, and up into the back of a truck which some builders had parked there. I have no idea how he got up into the back of that truck because it was farther off the ground than he was! But when I saw him, Ryan was trying to get down. He was hanging off the back of this thing from the waist downward, and his feet were still suspended about eighteen inches from the ground. I saw he was going to hurt himself. There was just no way he could get down. I came out the back door, slipped up behind him, and put my hands under him to catch him when he fell.

Ryan didn't know I was there. He didn't hear me coming, but when I got up close to him, I noticed he was talking to himself. He was probing empty space with one foot back there and saying, "Somebody help da boy."

"Help da boy" I did.

—Dr. James Dobson

NEVER BE SURPRISED WHEN YOU SHAKE A CHERRY TREE IF A BOY DROPS OUT OF IT; NEVER BE DISTURBED WHEN YOU THINK YOURSELF IN COMPLETE *solitude if you discover a boy peering out at you from a fence corner.*
—David Grayson

Hail to the Chief

The sound started as a low rumble deep in his stomach. It slowly began to build in intensity. Finally, a burp emerged from our son Zachary that would qualify for a place in the *Guinness Book of World Records,* in the "burps by two-year-olds" category.

Every parent worries that his child will do something like this perhaps in front of a neighbor or a prim and proper aunt. Mine chose to show his stuff in the presence of the President of the United States.

The occasion was my last day at the White House after serving President Reagan in a variety of positions for eight years. My wife and I, and our very excited children, had a few intimate minutes in the Oval Office with the President to say goodbye. Then we walked a few yards away to the ornate Roosevelt Room where a hundred close friends and colleagues gathered to wish me good luck.

The President, as is customary when a presidential assistant leaves, was saying a few kind words about me. Just about the time he started praising my work, our son broke the magic of the moment with his gastric surprise.

Fortunately, my wife was holding him near the President's "bad" ear so I'm not sure if the Commander-in-Chief heard the sonic boom. But he must have wondered why my hundred friends broke into laughter at the very moment he was praising my good work.

Oh well, Zach will have a great story to tell his children.

—Gary L. Bauer

Mother's Lap

The bond between mother and child is no secret, for it begins long before baby is born. Mothers have given their little ones life, and for this they are forever in her debt, constantly seeking new ways to please her and day by day showing her where their lives have taken them that day. A mother returns their love in many ways, depending upon who she is. She might plan a birthday party that's a hit for all the neighborhood children, or help heal scrapes with bandages and kisses. She might be a scientist who shows her little assistants the joys of bugs and butterflies. Or she could be a masterful storyteller who weaves nighttime tales of fairy princesses and curious frogs. But the best thing she gives her children, as she places them in the safety of her lap, is the special kind of love from the deepest places in her heart—the love of a mother.

NOTHING COULD STAY OR TURN HIM ASIDE, WHILE HIS MOTHER'S WORDS LINGERED IN HIS EAR. NO HARM COULD FALL ON A HEAD MADE SACRED BY *her blessing, and no evil enter a heart filled with such holy love.*

—Louisa May Alcott

Only Mom Will Do

I wasn't feeling well one afternoon, and I had decided to lay down for a while. My husband said, "No problem, honey. I'll take care of Ricky."

No sooner had my head hit the pillow than I heard my two-year-old call, "Mommy!"

My husband, with his sharpened parenting skills, took charge. "Now, Ricky," he scolded, "Mommy isn't feeling well. If you need something, Dad can get it for you. Just say, 'Dad, can you help me?'"

So, obediently, Ricky said in his best two-year-old language, "Dad, can you help me?"

Invisibly patting himself on the back, Dad leaned over to Ricky and said, "Oh, yes, Ricky, what can I get for you?"

"Get Mom!"

—Kim Jeppesen

HOME IS THE ONE PLACE IN ALL THE WORLD
where hearts are sure of each other.
—Frederick W. Robertson

Father's Arms

Father's great big hugs mean the world to little children. They run into his arms on many occasions—celebrating a victory, finding solace when the day didn't go quite as planned, needing just one more gesture of love before bedtime. In the loving embrace of a father, children find strength and reassurance that enables them to carry on with their projects and games. In a father, they also find the best kind of teacher—someone who patiently explains things and encourages hands-on practice, the kind of learning that sticks. Whether it's discovering how to reel in a fish or constructing a playhouse or mixing up a big batch of chocolate chip cookies, fathers encourage their children to join right in, learning and sharing in the comfort of an accepting embrace.

big hugs mean the world

to little children

encouraging

IT WAS THE POLICY OF THE GOOD OLD GENTLEMAN TO MAKE HIS CHILDREN FEEL THAT HOME WAS THE HAPPIEST PLACE IN THE WORLD; AND I VALUE *this delicious home-feeling as one of the choicest gifts a parent can bestow.*

—Washington Irving

A Child's Heart

My little girl, Jamie, who I still call Peanut, had just had her first defeat. She was cut from the gymnastics team. As soon as she walked into the house, my precious wife knew it was "Daddy time."

Little Peanut and I got in the rocking chair, and I just said, "Hey, Peanut, I spent my life on the bench. God doesn't care what team you're on. He just wants your heart."

Kids bounce back, like Silly Putty. In a few minutes she was out of there. And she was fine.

That night, after I tucked her in and said, "Good night," I was walking out of her room when I heard this little voice penetrate the darkness.

"Daddy..."

I turned around and said, "What, Peanut?"

"Thanks for tying my heart back together tonight."

I walked over to her bed because I wasn't sure if I really heard what I thought I heard. I put my cheek down by her little, soft, seven-year-old cheek of innocence. "Peanut, what did you say?"

"Aw, I just said thanks for tying my heart back together tonight."

"Darling, what do you mean by that?"

"Tonight, when I came in, my heart was broken. But you tied it back together again."

—Joe White

The Greatest Friendship

My oldest son Brady was gentle, frail, and non-athletic. From age six until third grade, he was the laughingstock of the soccer team. He couldn't walk and kick the ball. His teammates would send him home in tears, poking fun at his name: "Brady bunch, Brady bunch, couldn't kick a ball at lunch."

I had a habit as a new dad of lying by my kids at night and talking through the day. I'll never forget the night the greatest friendship I've ever known began.

Brady was sobbing on his pillow. "Dad, why do they pick on me like that?"

"I don't know, son, but one thing's for sure. I'm crazy about you, and I couldn't care less if you ever play sports again as long as you live. You might be an artist or a guitar player..."

"But, Dad, I want to play sports."

"Well," I reassured him, "you can do anything you want to if you want it bad enough. And buddy, there's nothing I'd like more than to help you get there."

"You would? I can? Do you mean it?" His teary eyes were filled with hope.

"Brady, make a goal, and we'll dream the dream together."

"Dad," he looked up at me with wonder and trust as only a child can do, "I'd like to start as point guard on the seventh grade basketball team."

I groaned inside but, somehow, knew that "All things work together to him who believes."

"Okay, buddy, but we'll have to work out together every day after school for the next four years."

We ran. We dribbled. We shot. We did pushups. We sweated. We cried. We stepped on each other's toes. We trained. We prayed. We discovered friendship.

I'll never forget the smile on his face as he dribbled the ball down the court to usher in his seventh grade basketball season—just the way he'd dreamed it. I was so nervous that I had to leave the gym. The game was tied with four minutes left. He threw the ball away twice in a row and missed a free-throw as his team lost by one point. He was crushed, but I poured out encouragement. It was a rough year, but for the first time in his life, Brady tasted accomplishment.

Our times together intensified. He continued to climb; I continued to encourage. He was a dreamer; I was a dream-maker.

Going into ninth grade, Brady shot over 60,000 baskets. I stood under the net and caught over half of them. And this year, it all began to come together. Brady played well, handled the ball well, played good defense, scored lots of points.

And my boy Brady, one of my best friends in the whole world, helped set the pace for his team—who went 19–0 this season.

—Joe White

BLESSED BE THE HAND THAT PREPARES A PLEASURE FOR A CHILD,
for there is no saying when and where it may bloom forth.
—Author Unknown

Living in the Moment

Children have mastered the living of life. They know the meanings of words like anticipation, surprise, and joy. They know how to feel emotions, to let themselves get completely caught up in the moment without one eye permanently fixed on the future. Children will count down the days until a coming event—the first (or last!) day of school, a birthday party, a summer vacation. While Christmas tends to sneak up on grown-ups, children faithfully count down each day on the Advent calendar, spending long afternoons wishing for snow or shaking the packages under the tree. Come summer, children know how to drop what they're doing and sprint to meet the ice cream truck, aware that it will only travel down the lane once that day. Tuning their ears to the precious moment, children live life as it was meant to be lived.

precious *children live life as it was meant to be*

FOR UNFLAGGING INTEREST AND ENJOYMENT, A HOUSEHOLD OF CHILDREN, IF THINGS GO REASONABLY WELL, CERTAINLY MAKES ALL OTHER FORMS *of success and achievement lose their importance by comparison.*

—Theodore Roosevelt

Daddy's Girl

"Daddy, what are Spoolies?"

"Well, they're little things that we're going to roll your hair on, Kathy. We'll put some of this lanolin on each strand and then, let's see...roll it up and then flip the sides of the Spoolies so each strand will be tightly in place. Wait a few hours, unpop the Spoolie, and presto!— fluffy hair."

"Have you ever done it, Daddy?"

"Well, no..."

"Ready, Daddy?"

"Sure, kid. Climb up on the stool here, and let's get this show underway. You can pay me later." Kathy threw her arms around my neck and kissed me on the cheek. Her light-brown hair brushed against my face, and her eyes danced with delight.

"We're going to have a good time together, aren't we, Daddy?"

I looked down into her face and hugged her up close to me and smiled. "You're going to be one of the prettiest little girls in church today. Daddy's going to fix your hair, and we're going to make it look as beautiful as ever."

"Thank you, Daddy."

Within an hour, the entire head of hair had been thoroughly soaked in lanolin. My theory in applying the oil was very simple. If a little is good, a lot must be better.

"All done?"

"Yup. See, honey, it wasn't hard at all. We make a great team, don't we?"

"Yeah, we can roll my hair every day."

I wasn't sure about her "every day" proposal, but there was a warm feeling, knowing that the two of us had made it through our first major project together. After a few minutes, Kathy climbed back up on the stool in the tiny kitchen and giggled all over in anticipation. I reached out nervously and took the first Spoolie in my hand, held my breath, and unpopped it. Then I slowly unwound it, so that the strand of hair could fluff and bounce, but it didn't. It didn't fluff, and it sure didn't bounce. The entire strand was one soggy, oily ringlet, from the top of Kathy's head to her shoulders.

"Please, Daddy, can I see how pretty it is?"

"Honey, why don't we wait a minute? Let's see if Daddy can just touch it up a bit. I've got a great idea. Why don't we find a pretty color scarf, and we'll tie your hair up in it? You'll be the only little girl in church wearing something as beautiful as that."

"Yeah, that's a real good idea."

In three days, most of the greasy lanolin had been washed out, and the hair had finally dried. On the fourth day, I plotted a new course. "Honey, how would you like to have short hair?"

"How short, Daddy?"

"Well, real short. I think that's going to be the new style, and you know that I want you to have the latest style in haircuts."

"That'll be great, Daddy. Let's cut it off, real short."

"Real short, honey. I promise."

—Bruce McIver

39

Through a Child's Eyes

Every now and then as grown-ups, we catch glimpses of our life as children. A familiar smell of soup simmering or cookies baking brings back a treasured memory. The waves crashing and the sun setting just so transport us back to the beaches of childhood. Why is it that the world seems so much bigger, so much brighter, so much more mysterious, to a child? Turning their bedrooms into sailboats or jungles, little ones are content to spend a good part of the time in the unseen world of the imagination. A child would rather create than compare; in playtime, nothing can be transformed into something. The novelty of experiences is fresh in a child's mind—the first hot dog eaten at the baseball park, the first taste of hot chocolate after sledding, the first refreshing feel of a cold pool on a hot summer's day. The world through a child's eyes is surely the grandest place to live.

A CHILD'S EYES! THOSE CLEAR WELLS OF UNDEFILED THOUGHT! WHAT ON EARTH CAN BE MORE BEAUTIFUL? FULL OF HOPE, LOVE, AND CURIOSITY, THEY MEET *your own. In prayer, how earnest! In joy, how sparkling! In sympathy, how tender!*

—Caroline Norton

Cooper's Bible

A while back, my little boy was just learning how to form words. He talked so cute and he couldn't enunciate right. I loved the way he talked.

I was on the road when I called home about 9:30 one night. My wife had just tucked little Cooper in bed. She told me his eyes twinkled and he looked up at her and said, "Mom, I want to memowize anuther Bible vuss so when Daddy comes home I can tell it to him." My wife was tickled to death. Cooper said, "Can you get my Bible?"

"Well, Cooper, it's dark." She knew he couldn't read anyway. "Let me just tell you one you need to memorize. This is a really good one."

"Okay."

So, he's sucking his thumb and rubbing his tummy when my wife says, "Cooper, a good verse to memorize is 'Children, obey your parents, for this is pleasing to God.'"

Cooper thought for a couple of minutes. He pulled his thumb out of his mouth. He looked at her and smiled. "That's not in there."

"Yeah," my wife responded, "it is."

He pulled his thumb out of his mouth again. "You just made that one up."

—Joe White

WHOEVER WELCOMES A LITTLE CHILD IN MY NAME,

welcomes Me.

The Book of Matthew

43

First Haircut

I just recently took my two kids to have their hair cut. My little girl was getting her first haircut, so I took pictures and made a big deal of the whole event. My four-year-old son saw how pleased I was about his little sister's haircut, and later that day, while I was on the phone at home, he emerged from the bedroom with scissors that had blonde hair on them—his sister's blonde hair. "Mom, you liked her haircut so much, I thought I'd cut it again!"

I nearly died.

Now I look back and I can laugh. One of the things I try to do is to take delight in the mischief of childhood. Sometimes you have to do that. When the toilet paper is running from the bathroom to the living room to the kitchen, you just have to stand there and say, "Where's the camera?"

—Kathy Hogan

EACH CHILD IS AN ADVENTURE

into a better life...

—Hubert Humphrey

44

Love Given

Love given from a child's heart is simple, pure, and nearly impossible not to return. Children let others into their lives with an openness that grown-ups would be wise to study and emulate. Looking beyond the outward appearance, children see into the heart. After all, a clown at a parade certainly is not dressed in the latest fashion, but little ones see the fun sparkling in the clown's eyes and wide, painted smile. They cannot help but laugh and rush up to give the character a hug. Children love in their uncomplicated acceptance of others. Little ones also have a gift for loving fully and completely, making steadfast alliances with the family cat or the best friend down the street. In giving of themselves, they receive like treatment, and the world becomes a radiant place.

the world becomes

a radiant place

WE FIND DELIGHT IN THE BEAUTY AND HAPPINESS OF CHILDREN
that makes the heart too big for my body.
—Ralph Waldo Emerson

Heaven Sent

Children do not come with an owner's manual, and well they shouldn't. Each little one is a special person all her own, each a gift from God, a package truly heaven sent. As we nurture and care for those entrusted to our keeping, may we always remember the wonder and blessing before us. And may we love and hug and delight in these precious little ones.

a package

truly heaven sent

BLESSED BE CHILDHOOD, WHICH BRINGS DOWN SOMETHING OF HEAVEN
into the midst of our rough earthliness.
—Henri Frederic Amiel